For all the Sophias.

Published in the United States
by Xist Publishing
www.xistpublishing.com
24200 Southwest Freeway
Suite 402- 290
Rosenberg, TX 77471

Hardcover ISBN: 978-1-5324-3168-5
Paperback ISBN: 978-1-5324-3167-8
eISBN: 978-1-5324-3166-1

Printed in the USA

xist Publishing

Wait, What?

Illustrated Puns, Jokes, and Weird Questions

AUDREY BEA

Illustrated by

ADAMM BUENO

If you wait for a waiter,

you become the waiter.

Ice skating is just walking in cursive.

If you get a bigger bed you have
more bed room,

but less bedroom.

You can't block out your sense of touch.

The word nun

is just the letter n doing a cartwheel.

‘W’ starts with a ‘D.’

If you clean a vacuum,

you become a vacuum cleaner.

Your fingers have fingertips and your toes don't have toe tips,

yet you can tiptoe, not tip finger.

If you sweat in a sweater,

are you the sweater?

A bathtub is just an opposite boat.

There was probably a royal taste tester

that got executed when a royal died from peanut allergy.

You don't hit the wall,

you hit the paint on it.

Horses run on their toenails.

Boomerangs are single player frisbees.

You can't change
the volume you
think in.

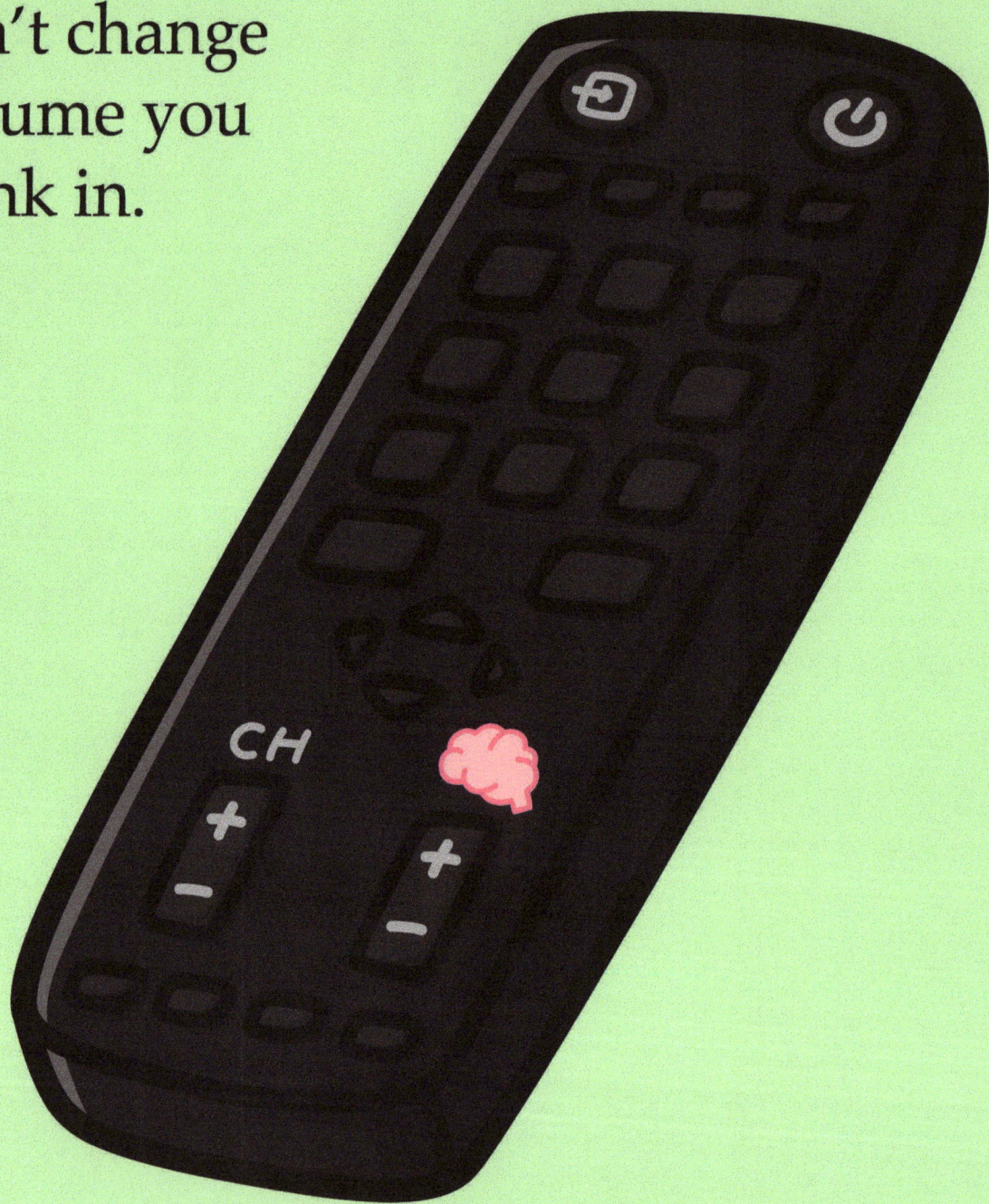

Ice skating is walking on water.

If you've found the best hiding spot,

you have not found the best hiding spot.

RENT - A - QUOTE!!!

SCIENCE PHILOSOPHY

SPORTS ARTS

Quotes are just borrowed intelligence.

You can't snap your fingers

inside your mouth.

When you brush your teeth,

you are just cleaning your skeleton.

Isn't it weird that we have a voice in our head that we use to read things,

hey look you're doing it right now!